DIVING AND SNORKELING GUIDE TO 🐚🐚🐚🐚🐚🐚🐚🐚🐚🐚🐚🐚🐚

Palau

D1026318

Tim Rock and Francis Toribiong

Pisces Books™
A division of Gulf Publishing Company
Houston, Texas

Publisher's note: At the time of publication of this book, all the information was determined to be as accurate as possible. However, when you use this guide, new construction may have changed land reference points, weather may have altered reef configurations, and some businesses may no longer be in operation. Your assistance in keeping future editions up-to-date will be greatly appreciated.

Also, please pay particular attention to the diver rating system in this book. Know your limits!

Pisces Books
A division of Gulf Publishing Company
P.O. Box 2608, Houston, Texas 77252-2608

Library of Congress Cataloging-in-Publication Data

Rock, Tim
    Diving and snorkeling guide to Palau / Tim Rock and Francis Toribiong.
       p. cm.
    Includes index.
    ISBN 1-55992-068-8
    1. Skin diving—Palau—Guidebooks. 2. Scuba diving—
Palau—Guidebooks. 3. Palau—Guidebooks. I. Toribiong, Francis.
II. Title.
GV840.S78R573   1994
797.2′3′0966—dc20   93-27894
                                                          CIP

Pisces Books is a trademark of Gulf Publishing Company.

Printed in Hong Kong

10 9 8 7 6 5 4 3 2 1

Table of Contents

Preface

For more than a decade I have been truly blessed to be diving the Palau Islands. Their reefs, walls, channels, and wrecks are unrivaled in the world. The saying *Palau has it all* couldn't be truer. By sharing my experiences and photos, I hope to bring to divers worldwide a sense of concern to help protect these most marvelous marine resources.

I have logged hundreds of dives with Francis Toribiong as my dive buddy. His spirit of exploration and adventure is the reason many of these incredible underwater discoveries have been made. He has always led an unselfish crusade to preserve and protect the rich natural and cultural resources of his homeland for the benefit of future generations. He has always felt it important for his countrymen and women to take a leadership role in the visitor industry.

Through this book, we hope to promote these marvelous dive destinations so Palauans may share with the world their culture and environment. I wholly support Francis' goals as we proudly present this coauthored guide for the enjoyment of visiting divers worldwide.

Tim Rock

How to Use This Guide

This guide is intended to bring to the diver the most popular and unique dive sites of Palau. Palau has it all: wall dives, coral gardens, drift dives, shipwrecks, deep channels, and tranquil lagoons. It even boasts marine lakes. "They're full of surprises, these waters here," Francis Toribiong often says when talking about Palau's incredible abundance and variety of marine life. After 20 years, Toribiong admits he hasn't seen it all, but this book will give the diver a major glimpse of Palau diving.

Aerial view of the Palau Rock Islands and 70 Islands National Park.

A diver swims along the 1,000-foot sheer dropoff of the Ngemelis Wall, rated by Jacques Cousteau as one of the best wall dives in the world.

To begin, approximate dive positions are shown on the maps of each section. In addition, each site is introduced with a chart that gives general location, most frequently dived depths, type of dive that can be expected, dominant marine life, and the logistical requirements. Palau has a population of about 14,000 people, many of whom fish and dive. Palau attracts a more experienced, traveling diver. The must-see dives are listed here; all of them can only be done with a boat and local guide. The extreme tide changes make currents run swiftly, so it is best to dive and snorkel with those who are trained and experienced with the waters of the region.

This book includes a variety of sites from the best snorkeling reefs to beach dives to the more exciting boat dives.

The Rating System for Divers and Dive Sites

A **snorkeler** is someone who is a strong swimmer and has had experience with ocean snorkeling. A **novice** is someone who is in decent physical condition, who is newly certified, who dives infrequently, or who is not experienced with ocean diving. An **advanced diver** is generally someone with advanced training who dives frequently and is comfortable with ocean diving. A **master** diver is someone at divemaster or instructor level or who has at least 100 similar ocean dives and is in good shape. We recommend that most of the wall dives and wreck dives be done by advanced or master divers. The currents can be tricky along the walls, so a diver should have the experience to properly compensate buoyancy. A wreck diver certification will be of great help to those wishing to see the shipwrecks.

Two things conspire against the diver in Micronesia: incredible clarity and strong currents. You will have to be alert for changing conditions and monitor depth closely. Before every dive you should consider the way you feel that particular day, your level of training, your physical condition, and the water conditions at the site. It is no sin to abort a dive. Remember the old adage: There are old divers and there are bold divers but there aren't many old, bold divers. Be honest in evaluating your diving skills.

The waters of Palau are filled with surprises.

1

Overview of the Palau Islands

Palau is well-known globally as a world-class diving destination. Located about 800 miles southwest of Guam, this 100-mile-long archipelago sits in one of the richest locations in the ocean realm. Not only is its sea life abundant, its islands are home to exotic birds, monkeys and graceful flying foxes.

Near the center of the country are the emerald colored, jungled Rock Islands. These magnificent mushroom-like formations provide a maze of splendid natural beauty and a protected haven for many rare forms of sea life.

Historically, the early Palauans lived an isolated existence. The islands were rich in resources and the Palauans practiced terrace farming as well as fishing and hunting. Remains of the ancient terraces can still be seen today on many Palauan hillsides. It is believed that because the natural resources on the islands were so abundant, the Palauans had much time to practice artistic skills, perfect building practices, get into politics and even war with one another. The northern and southern islands have been traditionally ruled by two different chiefs. That is still true to this day, as traditional titles are still held by individuals and clans.

Historians estimate there were 40,000 Palauans living in the islands at the time of the first European contact when Capt. Henry Wilson shipwrecked the *Antelope* on Ulong Island in 1783. The islanders lived in a thriving and complex society that was highly organized. As is still true today, women had an important advisory role and exercised influential control over land and money.

The British controlled trade with the island until 1885, then the Spanish took over until 1899. Christianity became a strong influence in Palauan lives. European diseases also took their toll. The population dwindled during the next century. By 1900, there were only 4,000 Palauans left.

The Germans bought Palau and the rest of the Caroline Islands after Spain lost the Spanish American War in 1899. German administrators introduced methods for stemming diseases, which were a Godsend to the decimated Palauans.

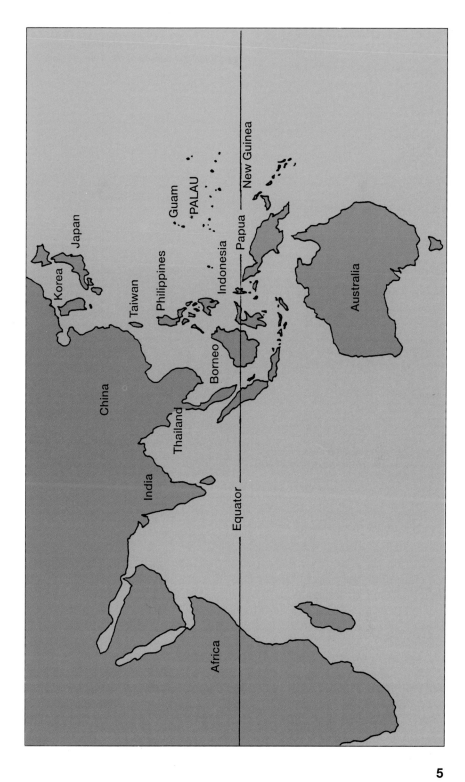

◄ *A craftsman works on the Koror Abai, the traditional meeting house in Koror and the symbol of the culture of the Palauan people.*

A small girl rests on what was once a Japanese water reservoir in front of her Koror home. ►

Japan took control of the islands in 1914 and ruled them until the end of World War II. They built the islands into progressive and productive communities that specialized in mining, agriculture, and fisheries. When the war came, the islands were also heavily fortified militarily. The islands of Angaur and Peleliu were the settings for fierce battles. The battle on tiny Peleliu lasted for three bloody months. A two-day air strike months before had sunk a major block of the Japanese fleet. War remnants of the strike still exist today. Koror was wiped out after the U.S. forces took control of the islands.

The job of rebuilding the intricate and productive Japanese infrastructure continues today, as the United States assumed a very passive role in administering the islands through the past four decades. The older people of Palau speak Japanese and sing Japanese songs when reminiscing.

Palau attempts to govern its people and to retain traditional values and roles by melding traditions with the progressive thoughts and politics of today.

6

Nature and Wildlife

Palau is considered one of the world's natural wonders, both above and below the surface of the water. Its immense barrier reef and broad landmass boast the second largest island in Micronesia next to Guam. As is the case with most islands, wildlife is limited but unique. Mammals are mostly introduced species and include monkeys brought in by the Germans to Angaur. There are lots of reptiles, including a species of saltwater crocodile also common to Papua New Guinea. Geckos, monitor lizards, two kinds of snakes, and some large toads are found. Insect life is also diverse; however there are no malarial mosquitoes here.

A pitcher plant survives and thrives on an arid hilltop in northern Palau.

A sea bird crosses in front of the noon sun at Angaur Island.

The islands represent two geologic happenings. The largest islands were formed by Eocene volcanic activity and are mainly composed of basalt and andesite. They have a high profile with an intricate stream system and a great diversity of plant life. The jungle is thick. It is impossible to penetrate some parts of Palau's interior. There is a freshwater lake in Babeldaob.

The Rock Islands are of limestone formation. Peleliu and Angaur are low platform and reef islands. Kayangel, to the north, is a classic coral atoll. The Southwest Islands comprise reef flats that have been subject to uplift.

Palau's marine life is almost unparalleled in the world. Because of its great diversity and the varied terrain, CEDAM named it one of the seven underwater wonders of the world.

The story of the Breadfruit Tree is a popular theme for storyboard carving.

Accommodations and Conditions

Palau has a new airport and is served by major air carriers. It also has first-class hotels and several dependable dive operations that are constantly upgrading their services and equipment. Arrangements can also be made through local tour operators to camp in the Rock Islands.

The U.S. dollar is the rate of exchange. A valid passport is needed for entry into Palau. Palauan, English, and Japanese are spoken here. The U.S. Postal Service carries letters for the same rates as it does in the U.S. mainland.

There are hotels for every budget and desire. Arrangements can be made to stay in local homes or rustic resorts on far-off islands or at first-class, every-amenity hotels right in town. Jungle tours to old war relics can also be arranged.

Tasting fine seafood cuisine in the many local restaurants is also a must. Sashimi, fish dinners, and local dishes are available at several places in and around Koror. If you find a restaurant you like, make arrangements for some mangrove crab.

Palau's waters support huge sea animals like the whale shark and the salt-water crocodile (an animal of Palauan legend as well). They also host a wide spectrum of fish and coral life. Virtually every dive promises something new and breathtaking. Visibility ranges from 50 feet to well over 100 feet along the dropoffs, and water temperature varies slightly from about 78° to 82°F. The weather is tropical. The rainy season is September through November, with showers possible starting in June. The trade winds start blowing in January and usually end by May. Temperatures vary from 76° at night to possible highs of 90° during the day, the average being around 86°. The night skies are incredible. Star gazers will go wild.

◀ The Marina Hotel offers waterfront living near downtown Koror with easy access to boats, diving, and dining.

The sheer drop of Palau's walls can be seen as the reef disappears into the blue water just feet from the boat anchorage. ▶

2

Diving the Dropoffs and Reefs

Two dropoffs have attracted photographers from around the world. One is at Peleliu, the other in the Ngemelis islands called Blue Corner. The entire southern end of the archipelago is blessed with world class wall diving, including impressive, coral-rich dropoffs.

Dive Site Ratings

		Snorkeler	Novice w/Instructor	Advanced	Master
Dropoffs					
1	Blue Corner			x	x
2	The Blue Holes	x		x	x
3	New Dropoff			x	x
4	Big Dropoff/Ngemelis Wall	x	x	x	x
5	Turtle Cove	x	x	x	x
6	Sweetlips Reef	x	x	x	x
7	German Channel	x	x	x	x
8	Peleliu Tip			x	x
9	Angaur			x	x
10	Siaes Tunnel	x		x	x
11	Ngerumekaol/Ulong Channel	x	x	x	x
12	Ngeremlengui Pass			x	x
13	Kayangel Atoll	x		x	x
14	Northern Wrecks	x	x	x	x
15	Short Dropoff	x	x	x	x
16	Tim's Reef	x	x	x	x
Rock Islands					
17	Wonder Channel	x	x	x	x
18	Jellyfish Lake	x	x	x	x
19	Soft Coral Arch	x	x	x	x
20	Coral Gardens	x	x	x	x
21	Chandelier Cave			x	x
22	The MMDC	x	x	x	x

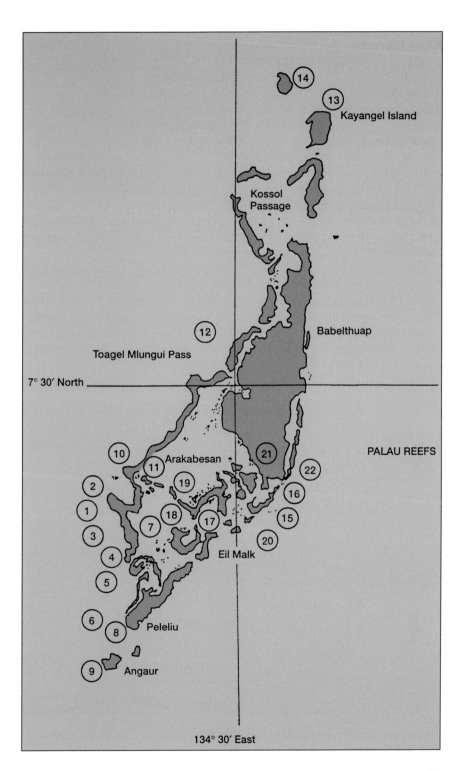

Kayangel Island

Kossol
Passage

Babelthuap

Toagel Mlungui Pass

7° 30′ North

PALAU REEFS

Arakabesan

Eil Malk

Peleliu

Angaur

134° 30′ East

11

Blue Corner

Location:	Ngemelis Island
Attractions:	Sensory overload
Typical depth range:	40–130 feet
Access:	Boat dive, local guide
Expertise required:	Advanced, master

Blue Corner, off the Ngemelis Islands, is one of those dives that is consistently electric, providing fish action in every imaginable shape and size. Large sharks are common, as are small ones, sea turtles, groupers, schools of barracudas, snappers and small tropicals, Napoleon wrasse and bumphead parrotfish, and even an occasional moray eel or sea snake. Incredibly big stingrays have also been seen here.

The amazing thing about Blue Corner is that about 90 percent of all of these animals are spotted on every dive.

The Corner is an area of the reef flat that starts in about 45 feet of water and runs for a great distance, jutting out into the sea before dropping off abruptly to form a wall. Small hills, sand tunnels, and gorges are cut into the upper side. A strong tidal current runs through, providing food for the bottom of the marine chain, which in turn attracts the middle and upper chain critters.

The crashing surf can be seen 50 feet above as a shark courses through the waters at Blue Corner.

Fish life along the shelf of the Blue Corner is prolific with a variety of schools, including jacks.

A typical dive starts by descending along the wall through schooling fish and at least a dozen reef sharks who are curious about the noise of the diver's bubbles. Prior to the tip is a cut in the wall that boasts immense gorgonian fans as well as feathery black coral trees.

Once up on the 50-foot level, the schools of fish that course the corner can be watched for hours. Some schools actually mix together, with as many as four different species swimming in one dense formation. By moving a little farther into an area of heavier coral growth, it is not unusual for a diver to see hawksbill sea turtles grazing on hydroids. On one dive, I counted six in a matter of about ten minutes.

Because it is so consistently active, the Blue Corner has become a mecca for world-class underwater photographers and should be considered a must for every serious diver. The currents here can be powerful and tricky at times. Be sure to watch for down and up currents that run along the walls and that can bring a diver up or down faster than wanted and really mess with a dive profile. The sharks here are well-fed, but treat them with respect anyway, especially during mating season in May and June.

Location: Ngemelis Islands
Attractions: Large, light-filled caverns
Typical depth range: 10–130 feet
Access: Boat dive, local guide
Expertise required: Snorkeler, advanced, master

It has become popular of late to dive through Palau's Blue Holes and then make a drift dive to the Blue Corner, as they are very close to one another.

The Blue Holes are holes in the top of the reef flat that lead to four vertical shafts that open on the outer reef wall. The diver can descend here and then drift down the shafts, watching the sunlight play with the hues of blues as the refracted rays dance through the water.

The walls of the holes have tubastrea and wire corals. Black coral, or antipathes, grows sporadically, especially near the exit below. These corals don't especially like or need the direct sunlight that other corals require.

The dive is quite deep, with the first exit at about 85 feet. Down this deep, the water is a heavy blue that goes deeper and darker to the open sea. Incredibly large fish have been seen here, including some immense wahoo and some ocean-going tuna resembling silver Volkswagens.

The bottom is sandy. Spotted leopard nurse sharks have been known to rest here, allowing divers to approach very close before being coaxed from their resting spot. If the shark looks more like it has zebra stripes, it is a young

The Blue Holes can be seen from the air as can the famous point of the Blue Corner. Drifting from Blue Holes to Blue Corner has become a popular dive.

Competition for growing space on the walls can produce beautiful results, such as this sea fan and tunicates.

specimen whose stripes will eventually become spots. Whitetip sharks sleep here as well.

The diver can exit and when the current is right, drift all the way to Blue Corner, watching out for sharks and turtles on the way. Or it is easy to ascend and explore the outer wall, which has gorgonian sea fans and a rich violet soft coral that becomes a ruby red when exposed to a strobe light.

Saltwater Crocodiles

One animal no one seems to want to encounter while diving is the saltwater crocodile, which inhabits all parts of Palau. The number of crocodiles has dwindled due to overhunting spurred by one of the Trust Territory governors in the 1960s after a Palauan was eaten by a large croc. A series of "crocodile hunters" from Japan and Australia decimated the population. There are estimated now to be about 30 crocs in the northern Peleliu mangroves and perhaps the same number in the river region of north central Palau. There are about 40 on a farm near the KB Bridge on the Koror side, which is owned by a former croc hunter.

It was once thought that two species of crocodiles lived in Palau, but recent studies show there is only one type of croc. These animals are nocturnal and reclusive, so few people see them except some night fishermen who may catch a glimpse of their red eyes in their flashlight. They eat birds, fish, or anything they can get close to.

They have been seen sunning themselves in the 70 Islands Reserve of the Rock Islands and around Ngeruktabel. If you should happen to see one in the water, it would be best to get to the boat. If you're already in the boat, consider yourself lucky as they are easily spooked.

Saltwater crocodiles are found in the mangrove areas of the Palau Islands and are occasionally seen in the Rock Islands.

New Dropoff 3

Location:	West Ngemelis Wall
Attractions:	Great shark and 'cuda action
Typical depth range:	20–120 feet
Access:	Boat dive, local guide
Expertise required:	Snorkeler, advanced, master

The name may not be the catchiest, but that doesn't detract from the excitement the marine life provides.

For years, Palau's Blue Corner has been the premier attraction for dropoff divers. Move over Blue Corner, New Dropoff may just be your equal. The site is located right around the corner from Ngemelis or Big Dropoff, actually on the way to Blue Corner. Sometimes referred to as West Ngemelis Wall, the site is near the area called Fairyland, but features a steeper dropoff that starts in between 15–30 feet, depending upon where you jump in.

This area has a lot of currents, just like Blue Corner, and keeping yourself neutral can be a little unnerving when side currents, down currents, and up currents are all bouncing you around like a cork. But once you get a handle on what is going on, you can stop and appreciate the fact that the area is alive with all sizes and kinds of fish. A few lucky divers have seen a whale shark here.

Schools of grunts, gray snappers, and barracuda are common along the dropoff. There are many cuts and corners where currents propel divers. It is not unusual to go sweeping around a corner and find yourself within a few feet of silvery schooling 'cuda that are just hovering off the wall.

Most divers usually report seeing something special on this dive, including patrolling gray reef sharks that approach quite closely, graceful hawksbill turtles, and a school of snapper so thick it almost blots out the sun.

I saw a large, perhaps six-foot, leopard nurse shark swimming freely down the wall and out into open water. Usually, divers just see nurse sharks sleeping on the ocean floor. It was an exciting moment to see one in action as its swimming action is completely different from most sharks.

New Dropoff has its share of beautiful coral fans and soft corals as well. The wall is alive with small tropicals, and sea anemones are found along the upper reaches of the drop. The dive ends at an area where much of the tidal flow exits the inner reef flats and the water can be a little murky. During normal conditions, visibility is about 80 feet along this wall.

New Dropoff is one of the bottomless dives that has made Palau famous, so it is wise to keep a good eye on your depth gauge and realize what you're doing. It is easy to get carried away swimming after a turtle or some other exotic marine animal here and find your dive profile completely botched.

The top of the dropoffs is home to schools of tropicals such as these pyramid butterflyfish.

About Drift Diving

Drift diving is an integral part of Palau diving because tide changes can be as great as seven feet, although they average around five. With the volume of waters flowing in and out of the channels, across the reefs, and along the walls, the currents become the diver's buddy, helping propel him or her through the water with amazing ease. This saves on air and energy and gives the diver the incredible sensation of flying. It is a good way to go, especially if you're not taking pictures.

Trying to grab on to something and struggle to take a photo in a current usually results in two things: a bad picture and some broken coral. Look and think ahead. You can be moving at one knot or more, pretty fast for a land mammal, so take care not to crash into anything or grab and break off coral. Nasty cuts can result from a coral crash.

On the walls, especially places like Blue Corner, New Dropoff, and Peleliu Tip, there can be up and down currents to complicate your drifting. Keep an eye on your computer and a hand on your buoyancy button to compensate. Occasionally, a current will act like a gusty wind when it picks up steam for a while and then becomes almost nonexistent.

The best bet is to stick with your Palauan dive guide. These guides are among the best drift and wall divers in the world and will keep you out of trouble so you can enjoy the free ride.

Colorful marine growth adorns the dropoffs around the islands.

Location:	Ngemelis West Channel
Attractions:	Sheer wall of life
Typical depth range:	3–900 feet
Access:	Boat dive, local guide
Expertise required:	Snorkeler, novice, advanced, master

Perhaps the most-fabled wall dive of sport diving lore is the Ngemelis Wall in southern Palau. This sheer cut supports just about every form of marine life divers hope to see when visiting remote ocean areas. Located just south of the historic German Channel, the dropoff starts in extremely shallow water (sometimes knee deep at low tide) and falls to depths greater than 900 feet.

The gorgonian fans along Ngemelis Wall are varied and colorful and start as shallow as 20 feet of water. A diver can to just catch the current and float by.

The feeling a diver gets after taking a couple of kicks from the shallow reef top and buoyantly hanging over the inky abyss must be similar to a sky-diver's rush. Normally, a gentle current runs along the southeastern wall, which is the most frequented dive area. A diver can dump the air from his BC and free float to just about any desired depth while experiencing a drift dive that makes swimming optional.

The wall has an abundance of sea fans at all depth levels. The deeper fans can reach nine feet across and come in hues of crimson and green. Crinoids sit on these fans to feed in the current and decorate them like holiday tinsel. The wall is also home to great barrel sponges and pretzel-like rope sponge formations.

The fish population is also quite varied. Big schools of yellowtails course the wall vertically, seeming to spill into the water from above the reef. The top of the wall is also rich in marine life with many sea anemones and clouds of chromis and small reef fish. For sheer beauty, Palau's Big Dropoff is hard to rival anywhere in the world.

Outbursts of brilliant red soft coral decorate Palau's coral walls.

Location:	North of Peleliu
Attractions:	Wall, blue hole
Typical depth range:	5–130 feet
Access:	Boat dive, local guide
Expertise required:	Snorkeler, novice, advanced, master

Across the Ngemelis Channel is an area fondly known as Turtle Cove. This is a popular rest stop for Blue Corner divers. There is a shaded beach and good snorkeling at the cove and, after the proper surface interval, a blue hole/wall dive is very handy.

The hole sits atop the shallow reef flat. At low tide, it is possible to stand at the edge of the hole with part of your body still out of the water. The next step is the fun part. Drifting through this hole, you will see red and yellow soft coral trees in about 30 feet of water.

The inside of the hole is honeycombed with exits at various depths. One small passage is the home for a family of large lionfish. They have lived in this little cave for years and are occasionally visited by a grouper.

Soft corals and sea fans greet the diver who descends Turtle Cove's Blue Hole.

This green sea turtle displays a crescent-shaped bite on its shell and a lost flipper, probably due to an attack from a shark or similar predator when it was a hatchling. It was photographed swimming in open water along Turtle Cove wall.

Drifting farther down, a large window opens to the outer wall at only 70 feet. All along this area are elegant, golden sea fans and wispy black coral trees. A leopard nurse shark sometimes sleeps on the bottom.

The bottom then slopes down to about 90 feet and falls off to more than 200 feet. The outer wall rises to near the surface on both sides and a swim along it will bring good marine activity. There are fans of burgundy and cream adorned with flowing crinoids. Fluted oysters also display their kaleidoscopic mantles until scared shut by a burst of bubbles. Schools of fusiliers and tiger-striped sweetlips add to the fish action.

The western end of this cove continues around a point to a wall that parallels Ngemelis. This is also a good dive, where the wall slopes instead of dropping off vertically.

Location:	Across from Big Dropoff
Attractions:	Wall, resting turtles, fish
Typical depth range:	10–130 feet
Access:	Boat dive, local guide
Expertise required:	Snorkeler, novice, advanced, master

Palau's Ngemelis Wall, also known as Big Dropoff, is one of the most-famed dives in the world. It is a sheer wall teeming with fish and covered with every coral imaginable.

Just a short ride across the Ngemelis Channel is one of the least-known dives in the world, Sweetlips Dropoff, near Ngercheu Island. The wall here is not as extreme as Ngemelis and the diver can go down along a sloping decline that features some relief areas full of corals and cracks that provide a home for a number of marine critters and large platter corals that sometimes become resting places for a lot of turtles.

On the first dive I made here, I counted 11 hawksbills during the course of a 60-minute, 60-foot submersion. I also saw many reef sharks, but for the most part they tended to stay deeper, at the 90–140-foot range, patrolling what was apparently their territory.

The wall has sea fans, though not of the immense size like those at Ngemelis, and large stands of leather corals with their soft, swaying tentacles that resemble anemones. Like many of Palau's spectacular reefs, Sweetlips starts in about three feet of water. Near the reeftop are crinoids in proliferation. They come in many hues, with some being brilliant combinations of evergreen, gold, and black.

The many cracks and crevices attract large groupers and a number of sweetlips, hence the name. Smaller reef fish like pyramid butterflies and schools of fusiliers are common.

Sweetlips Dropoff isn't the world's greatest dive, but it ain't bad either. When the seas are calm in southern Palau, it makes for a fine second dive and may provide some surprises as well.

A leather coral and a gorgonian sea fan intertwine along the wall.

Location:	North of Ngemelis Wall
Attractions:	Giant clams, corals, and rays
Typical depth range:	20–80 feet
Access:	Boat dive, local guide
Expertise required:	Snorkeler, novice, advanced, master

Heading north from the Ngemelis Wall toward the Rock Islands, divers pass an area of broad sand flats covered by 10–40 feet of water. The reflection from the white sand turns the sea to a bright shade of turquoise. This inviting area has been called the German Channel, named after the cut the Germans blasted through the reef to ease boat passage during the occupation of Palau from 1899 to 1914. This vast expanse had not been dived for sport until a few years ago.

Tide changes in Palau can mean a difference of seven feet at times. The water funneling over these flats reaches a respectable but not treacherous speed and the diver merely has to drop over the edge of the boat and go with the flow.

A tiny shrimp is incredibly camouflaged by the mouth of a pincushion starfish.

Peleliu by Land

A daily commuter flight goes to Peleliu, the scenic island that was the site of a three-month battle during World War II that resulted in massive casualties for the Japanese and the U.S. marines. Today it is a quiet place with scenic beaches fringed with ironwood trees, rugged coastlines with rocky outcrops, and a dragonback ridge that holds many monuments to those who suffered in the war.

The dropoffs around Peleliu are so steep that there is really nothing war related to dive here. But the land has many landmarks. The commuter flight flies over the Rock Islands and has to be the most incredibly beautiful flight in the world. The marine lakes and azure reefs around the Rock Islands and the southern dive sites can be easily spotted from the air and appreciated for their beauty and depth.

Once on land, it is possible to rent a car to see such sights as the **Japanese Caves** near the road by Elochel Dock. Small bats live here during the day. The battered **Japanese Communications Center** is downtown in Kloklubed village. **Bloody Nose Ridge** is the place where the fierce WWII fighting took place. **Orange Beach** was the invasion beach on September 15, 1944. Japanese bunkers can still be found here. At **Camp Beck Dock**, an assortment of old ships, including the one Gen. MacArthur used to tour the Philippines, as well as armaments and mangled planes, can be found bulldozed into heaps.

For relaxing, swim in the **Ngermelt swimming hole,** which is a sink hole with a ladder to help you get out after cooling off, or ask about a campsite at one of the beaches near the freshwater swimming hole.

The bottom appears to have been landscaped. Gorgonian fans with scarlet skeletons and snowy, white polyps quiver as they extend in the current. Crinoids in many hues abound on top of coral heads. Forests of staghorn coral thickets provide refuge for clouds of damselfish.

An observant diver can usually spot a cuttlefish in these thickets as well. They are curious by nature, resembling large squid, and they study a diver and react by flashing various hues of electric color.

Large triggerfish travel these flats, turtles like to sleep under the platter corals, and sharks pass by frequently in the distance. Many spots also have garden eels. Divers are often able to approach six-foot sand rays at close distance as they filter-feed in the current.

Big mantas are known to arrive near the mouth of the Channel in fighter-like formation at tide change, also feeding on the nutrients in the current. They can also be seen in deeper water, where the flats drop off to deeper water, as can grey reef sharks and other pelagics.

Cuttlefish find security in the beds of staghorn coral found along the German Channel.

Peleliu Tip 8

Location:	Southern end of Peleliu Island
Attractions:	High voltage drift diving
Typical depth range:	20–130 feet
Access:	Boat dive, local guide
Expertise required:	Advanced, master, drift dive

The southern tip of the island of Peleliu in the Palau archipelago provides a dive that is a true example of sensory overload. It is wild, open ocean that rarely sees divers, and the richness of Palau's waters is truly evident from the first plunge in the water.

The terrain around this end of Peleliu plunges abruptly to at least 900 feet. There is a shallow shelf that extends from the shore covered by 10–15 feet of water, but it ends at an abrupt drop in the form of a coral-covered wall that is alive with marine life. Normally, sharks are a fact of life along this wall. There are also turtles, sea snakes, large groupers, and schools of mastiff bumphead parrotfish.

It is not unusual to find large sharks in the water column at the current meld at the Peleliu Tip.

A memorial to those who gave their lives in the fierce three-month World War II battle is located on Peleliu Island.

In the area, huge gorgonians of all colors grow in as little as 25 feet of water and extend to the depths, seeming to grow in size as they descend. Feathery black coral trees with thick bases appear occasionally and soft corals, one with the most electric royal purple polyps I have ever seen, adorn the outcrops.

Brown barrel sponges are home to white sea cucumbers that comb the surface of the sponges in thick numbers. There are also cuts and crevices to explore that are painted with encrusting sponges and tunicate colonies.

One note of caution, the current can shoot a diver upwards 40 feet in a matter of seconds and take a diver down just as quickly. This is a place to be vigilant of time and depth. The current is also swift at the surface. Make sure your boat driver knows you are up. Carry a signal float so you don't wind up floating to the Philippines.

These few concerns aside, which are just common sense when diving where two ocean currents meet, enjoy the exciting dive. Peleliu Wall has to rank as one of the world's finest sport dives.

◀ *Large and lush, sea anemones house resident clownfish, crabs, and shrimp at Peleliu Tip.*

Angaur 9

Location:	Southern archipelago
Attractions:	Pelagics, schooling fish
Typical depth range:	20–100 feet
Access:	Boat dive, local guide
Expertise required:	Advanced, master

   Angaur is not dived much by sport divers because the open ocean crossing between Peleliu and Angaur must be attempted only when weather is very calm. The channel between the two islands can be very rough and the wave action on the western shores can be notable as well.

A sea fan adorns the dropoff at Angaur's Tip.

Angaur by Land

The commuter flight goes to Angaur daily, a ruggedly beautiful little island with a population not much over 200. This island is great to drive, ride a scooter, bicycle around, or hike. You will need water or sodas for all.

There are wild macaque monkeys here, the ancestors of escaped German pets, who are not in good graces with the local residents as they steal things from the back porches, clotheslines, and gardens. Mostly the monkeys hide in the jungle between the Santa Maria Corner and the old phosphate mines. There are fantastic blowholes near the mining area coastline. The path around the island is well-shaded in many places and idyllic. There are sandy beaches, some still with remnants of amtracs from the U.S. landing there. Angaur also has a place called Ngadalog Beach, where legend has it the souls of deceased Palauans go before they pass through to the next world.

Blowholes spew geysers along Angaur's rugged western coastline. This island is also home to the only wild monkeys in Micronesia.

Like Peleliu, Angaur also has numerous remnants of World War II on its beaches and in its jungles, such as the wreckage of this huge airplane.

One place people dive is at the Santa Maria Corner along the northeast shore. Actually, there is a Catholic shrine to the Blessed Virgin, a Buddhist monument, and a Shinto Shrine here—this is also a popular corner for religions.

This site slopes quickly to 90 feet and offers some extremely clear water. Angaur is the top of a submerged mountain. It rises from the sea with little in the way of protective fringing reef. The wave action here is intense. Thus, the coral heads are small at reeftop. Down deeper, expect to see sea fans and lots of fish. The schools of fish here can be quite large at times, with a mixture of pelagic fish including whale sharks and even oceanic whitetips and tiger sharks. Diving here can be an adventure and a unique entry in your dive log, but the better diving is still farther north where the coral attracts more sea creatures.

Location:	West of Ulong
Attractions:	Huge, coral filled cavern
Typical depth range:	80–130 feet
Access:	Boat dive, local guide
Expertise required:	Advanced, master

The Siaes Tunnel, located along Palau's outer barrier reef west of the Ulong Channel, is one of the most exciting dives these islands have to offer. It was found quite by accident by one of Francis Toribiong's guides a few years ago. A gaping cavern known for its sheer wall and active marine life, this mammoth underground cave is the home for a multitude of sea inhabitants from wispy black coral trees to sleeping sharks.

The tunnel entrance is not visible from the surface. Boats normally anchor in about 15 feet of water at the dropoff. The diver drifts down through the resident population of pyramid butterflyfish and begins descent along this active wall.

Siaes Dropoff is a fine experience in itself. The gorgonian fans in the hues of electric crimson and sun gold quiver in the current that runs gently along the wall. Schools of weighty bumphead parrotfish course the area, moving vertically along the cliff face. At around 60 feet, the entrance to the tunnel becomes apparent.

A delta of sand comes clearly into view at this point. Unlike most of the wall, which drops off to awesome depths, the bottom here is visible. At about 90 feet, the mouth of the chasm is clear and inviting to the curious diver.

Exploring this tunnel is not child's play by any manner. At depths averaging 100–130 feet, the cave provides an experience that borders on the edge of safe sport diving. Any misgivings about equipment not being in top shape or the steadiness of a dive partner should be strong factors in choosing to make this dive at a time when you are better prepared. It can be a long way out and a long way up in case of an emergency.

If all systems are go, a look inside should garner some high voltage surprises. It is not unusual to see a large ray rising from the sandy bottom of the entrance. Inside, reef and whitetip sharks use the cave for a resting place. They can be approached closely if care is taken not to breath too heavily. A school of crevalle jacks is usually present and swoops in to satisfy its collective curiosity past the diver's probing light. A Jewfish-sized grouper has also been reported here. The roof of the cave is forested in black coral, while the floor is covered in gorgonians.

Sharks also like to sleep in a side opening of the tunnel. This room, found to the right while exiting, is at a more respectable 100 feet and also has a window exit to the sea. A diver can swim to it using natural light, but a dive light is helpful here as well. The dark reaches are home to a moray eel and usually a sleeping leopard nurse shark. They are sometimes joined by whitetips.

The exit is made through a litter of large sea fans growing from the roof and the sides of the window. Ascend up the wall for a safety decompression stop.

Divers descend the mouth of the fan-filled shallow entrance of the first cave at Siaes Tunnel.

Location: West of Ulong Island
Attractions: Lettuce corals, groupers, drift dive
Typical depth range: 20–80 feet
Access: Boat dive, local guide
Expertise required: Snorkeler, novice, advanced, master

This pass near Ulong Island provides one great ride past underwater terrain that appears to be landscaped.

Ulong Island is the kind of tropical paradise a person would like to come upon if shipwrecked. It has beautiful sandy beaches, tall coconut trees, and

The Ulong Channel is famous for its huge stands of lettuce corals that house anemones and other invertebrates.

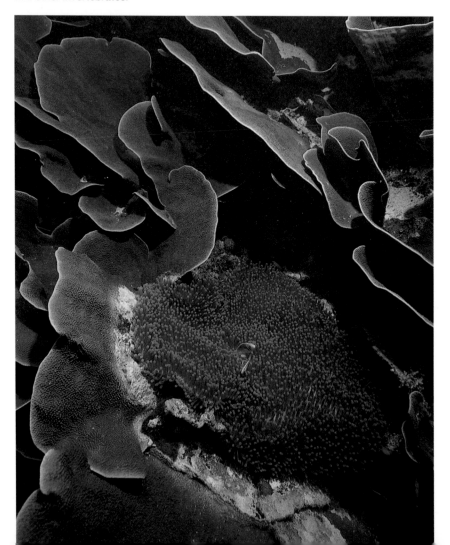

rich, green vegetation. Large cliffs loom up, protecting the flora, and birds soar through the skies.

Underwater nearby Ngerumekaol Pass is one of the best drift dives Palau has to offer. Dotted with huge coral heads and steep slopes on each side, the soft and fan coral cover appears to have been placed by a landscaping expert. Brilliant crinoids and jet black ones sit out in the daytime to filter feed. Big and occasionally exotic fish, like the spectacular threadfin pompano that usually inhabit open ocean, frequent this spillway. It is the spawning grounds for large groupers and a popular resting place for hawksbill turtles.

Whitetip and grey reef sharks are commonly seen, and more than one diver has had a pesky remora try to attach itself during a channel dive.

One of the largest stands of lettuce corals you'll ever see is in the middle of this pass. Anemones nestle inside and, at night, beautiful basket starfish come out and catch particles in the current from the edge of the coral lips.

Ngerumekaol averages about 50–60 feet but can get as deep as 80 feet in some spots. It is normally an ideal second dive and an exciting night dive as well. Many divers prefer to drift out and go along the wall past the mouth. Monstrous, large groupers have been seen here.

The pristine Ulong Island beach is a favorite stopping place for divers for lunch and snorkeling.

Location:	West, central Babelthuap
Attractions:	Channel diving, abundance of fish
Typical depth range:	20–120 feet
Access:	Boat dive, local guide
Expertise required:	Advanced, master, drift dive

It is hard to beat the sheer excitement of Palau's Blue Corner or Peleliu Tip, but Ngeremlengui Pass is an exciting drift dive that provides the diver with a variety of undersea experiences all in one dive.

This pass is located about one-third of the way up the western coast of Babeldaob, which is Palau's largest and highest island. It is also the second largest island in Micronesia next to Guam. The pass is near an area where two large rivers empty into the ocean. The rich nutrients from the river feed

The very fortunate diver may be able to glimpse a dugong, or Palauan sea cow, in this channel. This is the only known underwater photo of a Palauan dugong, which shows its powerful tail and collection of large remoras.

the expansive mangroves that are the center of juvenile marine growth. The result of this mangrove hatchery is a great variety of marine animals that live in the nearby channel. The nutrients also feed the corals and create large growths of sea fans, tall stands of evergreen cup corals, and brilliant soft corals that grow in a variety of hues. The mangroves are also the main home of Palau's crocodiles.

The current runs swiftly here most of the time. This should be regarded as a drift dive and the diver should have an experienced boat driver who knows the reefs and can follow bubbles to pick up divers.

The wall along the pass ranges from a sharp slope to a total vertical drop most of the time. There are even places along the wall that are undercut, providing overhangs that have sea fans and black coral trees. While these walls are current swept and not as thick in growth as places like Ngemelis (Big Dropoff), they have a good variety of invertebrate life, sea whips, crinoids, anemones and all of those critters that like to filter feed in currents.

There are sites along the wall, especially between the two red channel markers, that have sandy slopes.

On one dive with some scientists doing survey work for marine resources, a school of striped snappers appeared and just kept coming. It was quite a sight to see as fish streamed by for what must have been ten minutes or more. The experts estimated that the school comprised at least a couple of thousand fish.

Many kinds of fusiliers also like these walls. Brilliant yellowtails and electric blues course by at the outcroppings, providing a show of motion and color. Larger sharks, Napoleon wrasses, and dogtooth tuna also swim by in the blue or below on the channel floor.

The grey reef sharks can be very territorial here and not as laid back as those along the Blue Corner. If they start giving a territorial display, get out of their territory by slowly ascending to a shallower depth.

This has been the only place that a mesekiu, or Palauan dugong, has been photographed underwater. These sea cows are similar to Florida manatees but have been hunted in the past and have adapted to open ocean for resting during the day to avoid predation. At night they come into the shallows to munch on sea grasses. The one I photographed had at least six remoras attached to its back and a school of yellow-stripe pilotfish at its nose swimming like mad.

Rarely dived but wild and full of surprises, Ngerlemengui Pass has large gorgonian fans that can dwarf a diver. ▶

Location:	North of Babelthuap
Attractions:	Classic coral atoll
Typical depth range:	1–130 feet
Access:	Boat dive, local guide
Expertise required:	Snorkeler, novice, advanced, master

Even on the best of days, this atoll is rarely dived because it is an extremely long haul from Koror. When the ocean is flat calm, it still takes a high-powered boat about three hours to get to the main island. Just when the last glimpse of land in northern Babeldaob Island disappears from sight, the first glimpse of Kayangel appears.

On calm days, its rugged charm is striking to even the most jaded island traveller, with the clouds reflecting off the azure waters of the languid inner lagoon. Four coconut-lined islands make up the atoll.

Only a little more than a hundred people live on Kayangel, which was wracked by a major typhoon in 1991. The waves caused some damage to the corals, but the snorkeling within the lagoon still remains a pleasant experience.

The diver is at the mercy of the seas and the weather here. Conditions can change quickly in the open ocean. Turtles are a common sight outside the lagoon. At the southeast side of the big island there are very deep, black coral-filled blue holes. Large table corals are common at Kayangel's best dive sites as are actual schools of groupers, a natural occurrence rarely seen anywhere.

This is a good place to see corals, a great place to see fish.

The most relaxed way to see Kayangel is to visit the untouched beaches, bring a lunch and snorkel til you drop. Overnight excursions can be arranged for those who want to really get away from it all. Bring your own food along and perhaps some presents for the chief, like coffee or a package of ramen as a gesture of goodwill.

The scenic islets of Kayangel Atoll have been a favorite subject of both above and underwater photographers.

Location:	Ngaruangel Atoll
Attractions:	World War II wreckage
Typical depth range:	2–30 feet
Access:	Boat dive, local guide
Expertise required:	Snorkeler, novice, advanced, master

North of Kayangel atoll is another partially submerged atoll that is the resting place for ships sunk during the war. One ship is the *Samidare,* a Japanese fleet destroyer, found and identified by Klaus Lindemann and Francis Toribiong with the help of Kayangel chief Radochol Rulukel in 1990.

The ship had grounded in August 1944 and was later sunk. It has been totally salvaged with the exception of some massive parts. There are two large propeller shafts, parts of the turbine housing, some gun barrels, a fire extinguisher, a machine gun, some plating, and some shells next to a large chain.

The stone money quarries in the Rock Islands still have some pieces of money that never made it to Yap, such as this immense 14-foot diameter disc.

The surrounding reef is a surf zone, not too abundant with major growth, but deeper water produces some nice hard corals and scattered anemones. There are also some curious grey reef sharks that want to know what's up, as divers probably only come here a couple of times a year at most. The chief says there were other ships salvaged in the area as well. Those remain to be found and positively identified.

Stone Money Caves

Stone money is the largest currency in the world and unique to the islands of Yap. It originated in Palau and transporting it was a task for only the stout of heart. The tale of the stone money of Yap is one of the most unique of any Pacific island story. Stone money to the Yapese is what gold is to many other people in the world. It is the ultimate treasure. What makes it unique is that its value is not determined by weight or size, but by its history.

If you would like to see an example of stone money, visit the cave on the Koror side of the Palau Islands that still has a large disc that had been hewn from the cave's limestone wall. The cave is said to have been used as a shelter by quarry workers, who would cross the channel on rafts and small canoes to some rock islands in Airai State where the stone money was quarried.

There, it takes some cautious stepping to negotiate the precarious footing up the steep sides of the island. Grasping a few sturdy roots and vines to steady oneself along the narrow path is a must. A thick-soled tennis shoe is the key to exploring in comfort. As you head up the washway that was used as a path to the quarry site, you will find the jungle floor is still littered with many shells. Workers apparently came down here to eat. Judging from the jungle floor, clams and other mollusk were an important part of the diet.

In a clearing lit by a single ray of sunlight sits the first vestige of days gone by. A huge stone money disc, over twelve feet across, rests on the jungle floor. Covered with decomposing vegetation, this is clearly one disc that never made it all the way to the bottom of the trail. Immense in size, a dozen men would have had to attempt loading this disc. These amazing stone money discs can be found only here and on northern Yap Island.

A nautilus shell reflects against the surface of an inshore lagoon. Palm trees and blue sky on the surface can be seen through the clear waters. Live nautilus are native to Palau and live in very cold water at depths of 600 to 800 feet. ▶

Location:	Short Dropoff, Palau
Attractions:	Coral fans, schooling fish
Typical depth range:	10–130 feet
Access:	Boat dive, local guide
Expertise required:	Snorkeler, novice, advanced, master

Short Dropoff got its name mainly because it is just a short boat ride from Koror. Located near a cut in the outer barrier reef on the archipelago's east side, Short Dropoff provides a great variety of coral life ranging from broad gorgonian sea fans to platters of hard corals of intricate patterns.

It is common for this site to be the first dive of newly arriving divers. Because many of those who travel to Palau are hard-core types who want to hit the water the minute they deplane, the convenience of having this sloping wall so close to the main hotels around Koror is taken advantage of by tour operators. The ride to the reef can take divers through the channel and across an open expanse to the reef. If it is high tide, however, an alternate route through the Rock Islands is the way to go. Ask your guide to take you this way so you can experience the greenery and winding waterways found here.

Located only a short boat ride from Koror, Short Dropoff is full of varied coral life.

Huge gorgonian fans like this one are a common occurrence.

Once at the dive site, a quick snorkel will reveal an upper flat reef crowded with corals and tons of reef tropicals. Silver chromis abound here as do wrasse, butterflyfish, and parrotfish. Many colorful encrusting sponges line the underside of many coral heads, painting them in oranges, reds, and royal purples. Tunicate colonies also attach themselves and delicate lace corals fill the fissures of many rocks.

This garden gradually slopes down to about 25 feet and then drops off abruptly. In some spots it is a sheer wall, but in other places, it slopes steeply down. The diving here is usually done on the protected inner reef wall. The depth can be whatever the diver wants, but there are many incredibly large golden sea fans, sponges, and branching corals at the 40–50 foot mark, making it quite safe for a long, exploratory dive.

It is likely that some of the first divers in a group will encounter hawksbill turtles resting on the ledges or munching on some hydroids. Throughout the dive, schools of yellowtail fusiliers will appear from above and below and swim by curiously. Short Drop is not known for its sharks, but, trust me, they are here too. Short Drop is fine for wide angle and macro photography as well. It is a great way to start a week of diving in Palau by getting a taste for wall and drift diving.

Location:	Near Mutremdiu, Palau
Attraction:	Variety of corals, sunken Zero Fighter
Typical depth range:	5–70 feet
Access:	Drift dive, local guide
Expertise required:	Snorkeler, novice, advanced, master

Very few people dive here, but I think Tim's Reef is a marvelous place to dive and snorkel. It is located about half the way out to Short Dropoff and features a somewhat circular reef surrounded by a couple of channels that are full of life. The best location is on the southwest side. The top of the reef has many small table corals in shallow waters that are home to many colorful tropicals. There are many holes, cracks, and small crevices that provide shelter for the fish.

Divers can go down the slope to staghorn coral flats that have lots of chromis. In about 60 feet there is a very intact Japanese Zero that was shot down in a World War II fight. It is sitting on its top. The guns and wings are still in place. A look underneath to the cockpit will reveal small glassy sweepers in a large school. Eagle rays have also been seen in schools here.

This site combines history with a beautiful reef. It is one of my favorite spots. In fact, diving all around Tim's Reef is fun and presents many surprises.

A diver looks under the wing of the Zero fighter at Tim's Reef to see the school of sweepers that make the sea floor come alive.

Beautiful hard coral formations in the shallows of Tim's Reef make this a picturesque spot for snorkelers and divers.

The Rock Islands

The Rock Islands range for 23 miles, starting near Airai State and extending down to Peleliu. They were formed when limestone coral reefs were lifted above the sea level. Up top, vegetation gradually took hold. At sea level the lapping of wave action and an animal called the iron-tooth chiton ate away at the islands' base, causing many people to describe the islands as emerald mushrooms in an azure sea.

The islands are very rugged because of their limestone nature, but many have soft, white sand beaches and some are equipped with shelters. There are even a couple of small hotels on the Rock Islands.

Diving here is pleasant, but the water is so rich in nutrients that visibility is not normally over 50 feet.

The islands are pocked with caves, grottoes, marine lakes, and coves. Some contain life forms and chemical mixes found nowhere else in the world. The islands also have great historical and cultural significance.

Location:	Wonder Channel, Palau
Attractions:	Variety of corals, fish
Typical depth range:	20–70 feet
Access:	Drift dive, local guide
Expertise required:	Snorkeler, novice, advanced, master

Wonder Channel, located in the heart of Palau's Rock Islands, provides a scenic drift dive along a sloping wall that is loaded with a variety of coral, fish, and invertebrates.

Because it is located in the nutrient-filled waters of the Rock Islands, don't expect great visibility. The numerous sea fans, crinoids, sponges, and other filter-feeding animals that make up the reef are here because all of the good things they like flow through the channel. Still, visibility rarely goes below 30 feet and can reach 80 feet laterally.

Wonder Channel is normally dived during tide change, which can vary as much as seven feet in Palau. This great flux and flow of water provides a swift current in many places that makes diving effortless and the actual dive a carnival ride through a coral wonderland.

Normally, one eases over the side of the boat and can feel the tug of the current. All it takes at this point is to drop down, become neutral, and float along for the ride. If something interesting comes along, there is usually sufficient coral cover along the slope to stop, avoiding the current.

The current moves swiftly through the Wonder Channel, providing nutrients for a wide variety of marine life.

Beautiful corals surround the bases of the Rock Islands, making them fine snorkeling sites. Live-aboards use the sheltered islands as overnight anchorages.

At the top of the channel the coral is mostly the branching kind, such as staghorn and elkhorn. Clouds of silver and turquoise chromis find haven in these formations. Farther down, sea fans and whispy black coral trees abound. Small hawkfish and pipefish weave through the lacework of the gorgonians and crinoids perch on their edges. Schools of yellowtail seem to swoop down from above or appear ahead. Many times they will become curious and encircle a diver.

Sea anemones and smaller invertebrates are also present for the macro photographer. Sponge formations resemble everything from Greek vases to rope sculptures. Small fish, not yet bait size, often seek shelter in the sponge forms. Add to this an occasional giant tridacna or green moray eel and one can see why Wonder Channel is popular.

Location:	Eil Malk Island
Attractions:	Marine Lake, non-stinging jellyfish
Typical depth range:	1–30 feet
Access:	Hike, local guide (bring sports shoes)
Expertise required:	Snorkeler, novice, advanced

Ever since the marine lakes of Palau appeared in National Geographic magazine, Jellyfish Lake of the Rock Islands has become a popular destination for snorkelers. Located deep in the islands, guides motor around nearly exposed coral patches to a shaded jungle cove. The water here holds giant tridacna clams that can be seen easily by snorkelers. A razor coral named for photographer Douglas Faulkner is also abundant here.

The excursion through the sharp, rocky limestone forest begins at the end of the cove. The hike to the lake is up a steep hill to the top of a rock island, then a snake down the ridges to the edge of a briny swamp. There are rocks out of sight here, so a slow, cautious snorkel out will prevent any scrapes or head bumping. The rocks don't give much ground, trust me.

The water will clear up and drop to about ten feet. Below, decaying vegetation mixes with a maze of roots. Small blackbelted cardinalfish dart in and out. A closer look will also reveal some small, white anemones with flowing tentacles lining the roots. The only enemy of the jellyfish, these anemones will eat juvenile jellyfish.

The jellyfish in Jellyfish Lake seek the sun and gather by the thousands where the sun is bright.

There are two types of jellyfish found here, the most prominent being the *mastigias* species. The animals have developed a symbiotic relationship with algae. Basically, the plants get their energy from the sun and the jellyfish from the algae. Thus, the jellyfish seek the sunlight to keep the algae producing. The animals have no need to sting as they have no enemies in this environment and they feed themselves. Thus, they are safe to touch.

To find the jellyfish, head for the sun. Depending upon the time of day, the jellyfish will be found in direct sunlight. As the sun narrows across the lake in the afternoon, the jellyfish move closer together and the snorkeler can expect to be surrounded by hundreds of thousands of the animals at all depths. Diving down into this sea of pulsing, gelatinous umbrellas and looking back at the sun is a surreal experience.

A word of caution. There are voracious saltwater crocodiles in the Rock Islands. Ask your guide if any have been spotted recently in Jellyfish Lake before hopping in.

The jellyfish have lost their ability to sting and snorkelers can dive through the animals without fear of injury.

Location:	Central Rock Islands
Attractions:	Huge soft corals
Typical depth range:	15 feet
Access:	Boat, local guide
Expertise required:	Snorkel

Palau's Soft Coral Arch is one of the few places in the Rock Islands where huge soft corals grow in assorted shades from vibrant reds to soft pastels, painting the sea floor like multicolored cotton candy.

The other sites in the Rock Islands that are similar generally lead into marine lakes and are difficult to access or else require scuba. But here, the snorkeler can see these corals, which feed on nutrients carried by a current that flows between the arched gap or 15-foot tunnel between the Rock Islands. This spot is recommended only for snorkeling as the soft corals are extremely delicate and fin damage and other inadvertent contact can easily kill them.

The soft corals at Soft Coral Arch have attained a variety of pastel shades that are a treat for the snorkeler and macro photographer.

Deep in the Rock Islands, a cave holds the bones of ancient Palauans who were laid to rest in the depths of this stalagmite-active cave.

Bone Caves

Located near the pass to Eil Malk is Yii ra Beldokel, which loosely translated means Cave of the Dead. In the ancient days, a group of people inhabited this area. These people took their dead to this cave and lay the bodies inside, wrapped in woven mats. Because their language and customs are different from the northern Palauans, it is believed these people later moved on to inhabit the far-away southern islands of Tobi and Sonsoral.

Today, Bone Cave can be visited by taking a boat to it, then wading in chest-high water for a distance to the mouth of the cave. Inside, a huge cavern opens up. There is no light, but that which spills in from the entrance. The remains of bones can be found along the walls and in the far reaches. The rear cavern is still active, forming stalactites and stalagmites.

If you visit this ancient site, tread lightly because the bones are fragile and unprotected. Most have been destroyed by sea water coming in the cave or by constant exposure from nature. Treat this site with the same respect the Palauans do, as this is a sacred area.

Coral Gardens 20

Location:	SE Ngeruktabel Island
Attractions:	Heavy coral growth
Typical depth range:	20–60 feet
Access:	Boat dive, local guide
Expertise required:	Snorkeler, novice, advanced, master

Several spots have been called the Coral Gardens because Palau is so rich in coral that there are many fine sites that both divers and snorkelers can explore. One of the best ones is near Ngeruktabel on the eastern coast. Competition for prime growing and feeding space is so heavy that corals grow over one another, on top of one another, underneath one another, and through one another.

Occasionally, a giant tridacna clam can be seen surrounded by all of this coral. Cramped, it can still open and close its immense shell, but some corals have attached to the outer part of the shell.

Schools of herbivorous fish descend on spots where algae or other tasty plants grow. The platter corals here are impressive, with some large tables.

Great, tangled thickets of staghorn corals also provide refuge for sea anemones and clownfish. At times, the orange rascals come out of the twisted protection to taunt a diver, retreating as the diver approaches for a closer look.

This spot is always good for a third dive as it rarely dips below 40 feet. Nearby are sandy islands with overnight shelters built by the Palauan government. These islands are a cozy site to build a fire and grab a bite to eat under the starry Rock Island skies.

It's not unusual for divers to see schools of tropical fish swim by for a look.

While extremely large tridacna clams have been threatened by poaching, the giant clams in the Coral Gardens have stood the test of time and are surrounded by heavy coral growth.

Location:	Rock Islands near Koror
Attractions:	Freshwater caves
Typical depth range:	10–35 feet
Access:	Boat dive, local guide, dive light
Expertise required:	Advanced, master

Chandelier Cave is a real departure from reef diving. Located in the Rock Islands near Koror, this shallow cave is made up of many chambers and a high ceiling that rises above the water level, allowing divers to surface, converse, and even take off diving gear and walk around in some of the chambers.

The entry is made at a small cove in the Rock Islands at about 20–25 feet through a jungled undercut. Take special care to stay up and away from the ocean floor. It is silt covered and stirs up easily. The light at the entrance is your exit reference, so it is especially wise to keep the water clear.

It is pitch black inside this cave without a light. There are stalactites and stalagmites to abruptly halt your progress, so don't even attempt to swim in without a dependable torch. Once inside, it is a limestone fantasy land, with an upper layer of fresh water that is crystal clear. The cave formations can be seen easily and a short swim will bring the diver to the first chamber. Here, huge dripstones hang from the ceiling.

The beauty of the inner cave combined with the water clarity gives the impression of unending visibility. A diver can get out of the water here and explore a small tunnel if the spirit moves him or her. In all, there are four chambers that lead back to a large area where divers can again doff gear, get out of the water, and walk around. The beauty of the dripstone and the chandelier-like formations make this a favorite novelty dive for many.

The underwater landscape around Palau can be breathtaking and full of surprises.

The Chandelier Cave features crystal clear water at the top of the inner chambers, making it an exciting novelty dive.

Location:	Ice Box, Ngemelachel
Attractions:	Giant clams
Typical depth range:	10–20 feet
Access:	MMDC staff member
Expertise required:	Snorkeler

The Micronesia Mariculture Demonstration Center is the world's leader in giant tridacna clam farming and development. The clam farming can be seen by walking along the big white runways that hold developing tridacna clams. The center also has a progressive hawksbill and green sea turtle protection and rearing program and several other ongoing projects that can be viewed for a minimal donation.

There are also some mature giant clams just off the MMDC dock. Ask permission, but it is an easy entry and a fine place to snorkel. These immense, decade-old, 600-pound behemoths can be easily observed. There are still some in the wild in Palau, but they don't like walls and dropoffs. You can see them here, in case you missed the sandy habitat they like.

▲ *The brilliant colors of underwater Palau are always a delight.*

◄ *The giant clams being farmed at the MMDC are the result of breakthrough mariculture research that took a decade to perfect. The patch reef in front of MMDC is an interesting beach dive site or snorkel.*

61

3

Diving the Wrecks

"A wreck is like a house left abandoned. Each has a story to tell. You have to look at it, figure it out . . . find out its past," wrote Klaus P. Lindemann, a German shipwreck writer who authored the book *Desecrate One, the World War II Shipwrecks of Palau* and who teamed up with Francis Toribiong in 1988 to find many new wrecks.

In piecing together the past, the team relied in part on the memories of Tiakl Boisek, who was a 13-year-old boy on his way to school in March of 1944 when the U.S. bombs began to drop. He was across an island channel from Koror and took cover under a tree while he watched as plane after plane advanced on the capital of Palau, bombing airstrips, buildings, and ships.

For two days, U.S. fighter planes, dive bombers, and torpedo bombers bombed and strafed everything in sight.

Dive Site Ratings

		Snorkeler	Novice w/Instructor	Advanced	Master
The Wrecks					
23	Iro			x	x
24	Gozan Maru		x	x	x
25	Kibi Maru	x	x	x	x
26	Amatsu Maru			x	x
27	Chuyo Maru			x	x
28	Seaplanes	x	x	x	x
29	Kiku Destroyer				x
30	The Refer	x	x	x	x
31	Channel Marker Ship			x	x
32	Helmet Wreck			x	x

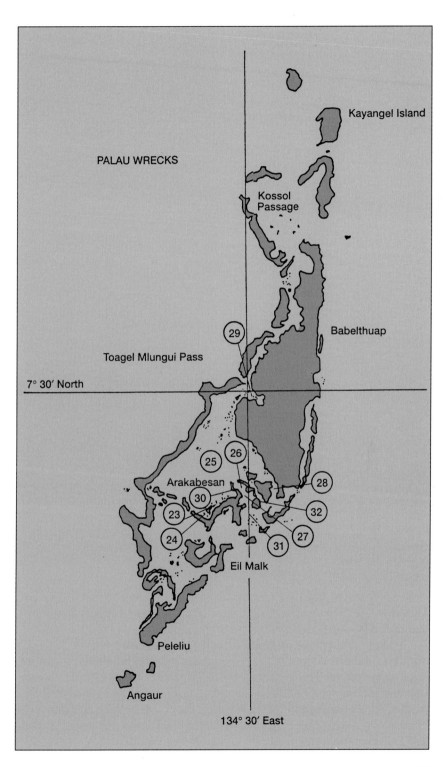

PALAU WRECKS

Kayangel Island

Kossol
Passage

Babelthuap

29

Toagel Mlungui Pass

7° 30′ North

25   26

Arakabesan

30

28

23

32

24

27

31

Eil Malk

Peleliu

Angaur

134° 30′ East

To obtain the same perspective as the attacking American planes, Klaus Lindemann (pointing) and author Francis Toribiong chart possible wreck sites from above Arakebesang Island.

To retaliate, the Japanese navy brought in all of the fighters it had nearby. They downed a few Americans, but more often became casualties themselves, outclassed by American aircraft and experience.

The American planes of Task Force 58 took a massive toll on the Japanese fleet. Malakal Harbor became a smoking inferno. For the most part, the ships went down at their anchorages in the lush Rock Islands. Some were salvaged in the early 1950s. But most remain fairly intact and good for diving. Nestled for the most part in shallow water, they have become artificial reefs, homes to massive schools of fish, bases for black coral and oyster growth, and undersea museums ready for controlled exploration.

Location:	Urukthapel Bay
Attractions:	Large, upright oiler
Typical depth range:	50–120 feet
Access:	Boat dive, local guide
Expertise required:	Advanced, master

The *Iro* is perhaps the best-known and most popular shipwreck in Palau. It is located just a short distance from Koror and is in an area that is normally protected from winds and rough seas. It is basically shallow as wrecks go and is beautifully overgrown with many forms of sessile marine life. Its sister ship, the *Sata* lies close by, upside-down, deep, and basically undivable.

Small schools of batfish are common on many of the wrecks, including the Iro, *where they follow some divers like a pack of curious puppies.*

The coral-encrusted mast of the Gozan is home to clams, oysters, sea anemones, clownfish, and hard corals.

The *Iro* was an oiler and a small oil slick can still be seen in the area as some form of petroleum product continues to leak after all of these years. It doesn't seem to hinder the marine growth on the ship, however. The first thing the diver notes upon descent is the schooling yellowtails around the masts. The crossmembers are heavily encrusted with hard corals and oysters. Smaller chromis also congregate here.

Divers are likely to be greeted by a resident school of batfish that aren't at all shy. My guess is that they wisely follow divers because scuba fins probably kick up sediment and expose meals, such as small shrimp, for the batfish to dine on. They are marvelous photographic subjects, faithfully following the photographer like a pack of puppies.

The *Iro* was built in 1922. It was sunk in March of 1944 and was also the subject of some salvage after the war. Many of the ships in Palau were salvaged in some way, and this is why places like the bridge areas are usually stripped on the sunken ships in this anchorage.

The *Iro* was the victim of a submarine torpedo attack prior to the Desecrate One air raid and her bow displays a large crescent where a hit took place. A diver can actually swim through this hole, which is now heavily overgrown with black coral and sponges. The thick anchor chain runs nearby and is also the home of marine invertebrates.

The bow gun is mounted on a huge platform. This, too, is overgrown with delicate, wispy black coral trees. It is an older gun with a calibre of 14 centimeters and a low trajectory.

The aft ship has a number of overgrown pipes, derricks and a beautiful mast configuration. The galley is also located back here, but it is pretty thick in silt and should be explored only by the prepared and experienced. Pots, pans and a stove are recognizable. They are in the tall deckhouse located in front of the poop deck. The aft also holds a large gun that is heavily encrusted with black coral.

Location:	Rock Islands
Attractions:	Reef-like corals
Typical depth range:	25–80 feet
Access:	Boat dive, local guide
Expertise required:	Novice, advanced, master

The *Gozan Maru* was discovered by Francis Toribiong while making an aerial search of the Rock Islands for dive sites and unique formations. It was found in 1984 and is very much intact. It went down on its side and now lists heavily to port. The shallow part of the hull closest to the surface resembles a reef. All types of corals have latched on to this wreck, from brain, platter, and star corals to large leather corals. Sea anemones are interspersed with this growth and come with a variety of clownfish. One purple-tipped anemone with skunk clownfish is especially photogenic. Small schools of a half-dozen barracuda roam this ship and at times approach close enough to be photographed.

Lionfish are colorful but their back spines are sharp and poisonous and should be treated with respect and some distance.

The flowing polyps of a wire coral catch nutrients on the deck of the ship.

The foremast has become a haven for all sorts of marine invertebrates. Tridacna clams nestle between corals and one-stripe clownfish are thick in large colonies of bubble anemones. Clams, oysters, whip corals, and bulb corals are all heavily congregated on the shallow mast. Schooling fish are thick, especially small basslets that make for colorful subjects for photography.

Swimming through the ship itself can be a little disorienting as it lists heavily to port. The deck is overgrown only by an occasional razor or Faulkner mushroom anemone coral. The holds are empty, but the second hold shows the damage that put the ship down. Klaus Lindemann surmises it was caused by a 1,000-lb bomb. The explosion apparently tore the bottom plates loose and the result is a jagged, inwardly bent, gaping hole large enough for a diver to easily swim through. Some water flows through here, as a large sea fan and other gorgonians, soft corals, and stinging hydroids have taken root. This ship is generally free from any noticeable current, however.

The upper bridge and rear are quite worthy of exploration, but stay out of the engine room. It is extremely dark, rife with pipes and loose wires, and disorienting from the list. A person can get into real trouble in there.

The aft has a fallen mast and small deck gun to observe. There is a ship nearby that is completely blown apart and the shock wave from this ship's massive explosion may explain some of the damage done to the *Gozan.* The nearby ship is the *Kamikaze Maru,* and it is really torn apart. There are some explosives on the *Kamikaze* still in what remains of the forward holds. This ship is best left alone. Instead, spend a couple of dives on the *Gozan.* It is worthy of the extra exploration and photography.

Location:	2 miles NE Palau Pacific
Attractions:	Open holds, corals, barracuda
Typical depth range:	45–90 feet
Access:	Boat dive, local guide
Expertise required:	Snorkeler, novice, advanced, master

This ship sunk while underway apparently trying to get out of Palau by heading north to the main channel. It now rests on its starboard side. It is subject to swells because the port side is only about 45 feet from the surface and is shaken often after big storms. Despite this fact, the coral growth is very nice around the ship's bridge and on the port side, with intricate platter corals sprawling broadly and small juvenile fish inhabiting the protecting cover of the lacey formations.

The engine room was blasted by salvagers, but it is open. It is still wise to stay out of it because the whole area is unstable. There is damage at the fore and aft of the ship. These hits apparently caused it to sink.

The reef around the ship, especially in front of the deck, is a pleasure to explore, with large stands of unusual acropora and platter corals. The mast has a lot of blue chromis busily flitting about, and anemones are found at various intervals. Blackfin barracuda schools, like those seen at Blue Corner, come in and swim at about 60 feet around the wreck, putting on a display worth photographing. On occasion a very large, solitary barracuda is also seen near the *Kibi*.

A lacy hard coral formation finds a home along the side of the Kibi.

Location:	Ngederrak Lagoon
Attractions:	Large Japanese tanker
Typical depth range:	70–130 feet
Access:	Boat dive, local guide
Expertise required:	Advanced, master

The *Amatsu Maru* is one of the newer ships sitting on the ocean floor in Palau. It was built during the war and sunk during the Desecrate One air raid of March 30–31, 1944. It is also one of the best wreck dives in Palau. It is close to Koror, located on the southern side of Ngerchol Island in Ngederrak Lagoon. It is heavily covered with corals, is a haven for fish, and still retains many of its wartime features because it doesn't seem to have been heavily salvaged.

This ship is often called the *Black Coral Wreck* and rightly so. The trees of the golden, wispy, low-light coral heavily adorn this ship. They are so thick that in some places they make it difficult to enter passages. The magnificently adorned lionfish *Pterois volitans* feeds on the clear baitfish that shelter themselves in the black coral branches. Lionfish are frequently seen in full display hovering over one of these coral trees waiting for a wandering fish to become its meal.

The *Amatsu* is about 500 yards long and deeper than most of the Palau shipwrecks. The deck depth averages between 90–110 feet and the visibility is not always the greatest. Some planning and thought is essential when exploring this ship. There is a machine gun on the bridge, although it has fallen into the silt. There are many places fore to poke around and explore. The forecastle can be entered easily and is spacious but can still be silty. A light is necessary while exploring.

The bridge has a large rail that is heavily covered with black coral as are some of the passageways. The passageways are passable but don't be surprised if you get tangled in some kind of coral. This ship is in an area that is normally protected and free of currents.

A diver checks out the marine growth on a wreck. ▶

Location:	Near Malakal Anchorage, Rock Islands
Attractions:	Heavy coral growth, fish
Typical depth range:	30–120 feet
Access:	Boat dive, local guide
Expertise required:	Advanced, master

The discovery of this wreck came when Francis Toribiong and Klaus Lindemann had been looking, searching, identifying, and exploring and were at the end of their safe diving time. Toribiong dived down to check out an echo that looked like a large wreck on the screen. The trouble was, no one locally had fished this site and the possibility of there being a wreck so close to a major population center was pretty remote. Resigning the sighting to some sort of phantom, Toribiong decided to ascend. As he picked up the anchor line and turned around, he suddenly encountered the imposing wreck.

As he explored the ship, he found it was incredibly intact. He found a 280-foot standard D freighter with its masts covered in coral and the wooden planking in some places rotting. But for the most part, the ship was truly spectacular to behold.

This ship is still in fine shape and is laden in coral and is a home for fish. The bridge is in 70 feet of water and it is 90 feet to the deck. The top of the mast is a garden of coral, sponges, and fishes. This is a fine dive that has a lot to offer divers.

The wooden floor of the bridge of the Chuyo Maru *has disappeared due to the destructive action of marine worms. The ship's telegraph has fallen and is partially covered with bright orange encrusting sponges.*

An air intake has become a planter of sorts for a marine garden of black corals, fluted oysters, and other invertebrates

Location: Southern Babelthuap, Palau
Attractions: Jake-Aichi floatplanes
Typical depth range: 2–15 feet
Access: Boat dive, local guide
Expertise required: Snorkel

The remnants of the *Jake-Aichi* floatplanes barely sit beneath the water on the Babelthuap side of the KB Bridge. Nestled between the Rock Islands, one is in fairly good condition, while the other has been exposed to waves and is pretty well broken up. The *Jake* was built by Aichi in 1938; therefore, these planes were virtually brand new when the war started.

These floatplanes had two principal roles. The first was to act as an attack plane. Each plane carried a crew of three and a cargo of bombs. The other role was as a long-range reconnaissance plane.

One of the *Jakes* sits near the cave where the last crocodile to kill a man in Palau was hunted down. The plane is scattered but the prop and engine are visible.

By far, the best *Jake* specimen is nestled across from the cave. The wings with little coral growth stretch out broadly. The engine has fallen forward, probably from its own weight, but the pilot's seat is still intact. The floats of the plane can be seen here as well, with one still in place under a wing. The metal of a sunken plane can be jagged, so take care when exploring these planes. It is best to come here at high tide.

A snorkeler inspects the seaplane wreckage.

Location:	Central Babelthuap, Palau
Attractions:	Shipwreck, corals, fish
Typical depth range:	2–80 feet
Access:	Boat dive, local guide
Expertise required:	Advanced

The ship believed by historian Klaus Lindemann to be the *Kiku Destroyer* lies in a channel in central Babelthuap. It may not be a dive for everyone as there can be tricky currents, low visibility, and a lot of wreckage, but for the adventurous, this dive is worth exploring.

The wreck starts on the shoreline at Karamadoo Bay, where shore hugging clams and mussels heavily encrust the shoreline and poke above the surface at low tide. Parts of the ship appear in two feet of water and cascade down to the bottom, which flattens out at around 70 feet and eventually drops deeper.

This wreck is broken but is still intact enough to probe. There is heavy silt, so care must be taken, but the openings provide areas to explore and sweetlips, snappers, large groupers, and other large fish use this wreck as a haven. The ship still has its stern gun, which sits pointing downward because that part of the ship is on its side. The 14cm shells sit on the sea floor nearby in what is left of the seaworm-eaten wooden boxes that once held them.

There is a lot to see at around ten feet if a safety decompression is in order. There is still some wreckage, and parts of the boiler and engine room are prominent.

Try to dive this wreck at slack, high tide because the visibility should be best, about 25 feet, at this time.

A diver inspects a cache of shells for the gun of the Kiku Destroyer, which sits on the silty bottom of Karamadoo Bay.

The Refer 30

Location:	Southwest Malakal
Attractions:	Baitfish, cooling coils
Typical depth range:	15–50 feet
Access:	Boat dive, local guide
Expertise required:	Snorkeler, novice, advanced, master

This poor old small, refrigerated coastal freighter was once draped with a large gill net that is slowly falling apart. Its aft was blown off during salvage, leaving the forward part of the ship open, with shafts of light flowing through the ship. This makes the ship easy to explore. It rests on its port beam, but it is so open that it is not disorienting to enter.

On the floor of the ship are the pipes that were used to cool the holds. Inside are delicate white antipathes trees that are homes to small cardinalfish and other delicate and nearly transparent tropicals. At the time of year these small baitfish multiply, the entire inside of the ship is a cloud of fish that move as a unit, staying just out of arm's reach of the diver.

The underside of the ship is covered with long wire corals. Prawn goby can be found in the sand below. This fish, in a unique symbiotic relationship, shares a burrow that is constructed by an alpheid prawn. The prawn, or small shrimp, builds a burrow in the sand, here very close to the hull, and the goby moves in. The goby uses its superior ability to detect danger and acts as a sentry for the prawn. The prawn seems to be constantly tidying its hole, moving rubble and particles out. The goby sits at the hole's edge. The prawn keeps an antenna on the goby's fin. If danger approaches, the goby flicks a fin and the prawn retreats, with the goby following if the danger, like a diver's macro framer, comes too close. According to fish expert Rob Myers, there are seven species of prawns that associate with gobies in Micronesia.

◄ *The refrigeration pipes of the* Refer *are found still intact in the forward hold.*

Location:	Malakal Pass
Attractions:	Ship, coral thickets
Typical depth range:	20–80 feet
Access:	Drift boat dive
Expertise required:	Advanced, master, drift dive

This ship is located in the channel near one of the channel markers and is referred to locally as the *Channel Marker Wreck.* It apparently was a Japanese fishing ship configured into a sub chaser, and it has large holds with coils that were used to refrigerate the catch. The gun from the small gun platform on the bow has been removed.

Today it sits at the bottom of a slope in a place with a swift current. When descending the slope you will see incredible stands of green tube corals. At night, the green tube coral polyps extend and are magnificent photo subjects. Take care with these as they can be jagged.

The ship sits at the bottom of the sandy channel at a slight list and looms out of the blue. It is large enough that, if the current is a problem, the diver can duck behind the appropriate side of the ship and be perfectly sheltered.

The deck is covered with soft corals and sea fans. Flurries of brightly colored tropical fish feed madly in the current that passes over the top of the ship. To watch their action, simply grab some part of the ship's frame and hang on. This is what the gloves are for. There are some immense angelfish around this wreck as well.

The rudder has disintegrated, but there are still three supports that stick out the back of the ship. The propeller has been removed. The upper cabin area is small but can be easily explored.

The shallow reef up the channel wall is an incredible dive all by itself. Cuttlefish huddle over carpets of staghorn coral. Silver, blue, and golden chromis live in these immense spreads of staghorn coral and feed with wild abandon, giving this reef a kaleidoscopic effect. There are numerous table and platter corals and some large sea anemones with their accompanying clownfish. There are also green, white, and brown tunicate colonies that spread for 30 yards in this filter-feeders haven.

If you don't feel like fighting the current to see the ship (the current varies from weak to ripping, so check the tide changes), a dive on the upper part of the channel on a sunny day is a marvelous experience.

The Channel Wreck *is one of the most popular wrecks in Palau because of its soft, hard, and fan coral growth, great variety of tropical fish, and close proximity to Koror, which makes it an interesting night dive.* ▶

Location:	Malakal Harbor
Attractions:	Munitions, war artifacts
Typical depth range:	28–95 feet
Access:	Boat dive, local guide
Expertise required:	Advanced, master

The latest discovery in Palau is a sunken World War II Japanese ship called the *Helmet Wreck*. This ship has been untouched and unseen by humans since the war. While positive identification is still in the wings, the ship is known as the *Helmet Wreck* because it carries a cargo of helmets that are now fused together from being in the ocean for nearly five decades. The ship sits on a sloping bank with the stern in 50 feet of water and the bow in about 100 feet. It is a new ship, as an inspection of its engine room shows a triple expansion, single shaft steam engine. Oddly, an inspection of the ship's coal bin (coal would have been used to fuel the engines and cook stove) shows little coal. The ship may not have been in use at the time it went down and may not even be Japanese built, but rather a captured vessel.

▲The boatswain's locker still holds beautiful signal lamps.

◀ Fused helmets, cemented by years in salty sea water, are just one of the war treasures found on this marvelous ship.

The ship has three holds, one in the stern and two in the bow area, with the ship's superstructure and engine room in between. The rear hold displays massive damage, the obvious result of a powerful explosion. The plating on the starboard deck and side was blown completely back, which caused it to curl until it almost touches the intact sides and deck of the bow. The bow-gun apparently was jarred from its mount by the explosion and lays on its side. The companion ladder and platform ladder were also doubled over and the mast ladder has fallen onto the gun platform. The mast crosstree is missing. The top of the bow mast extends to within 28 feet of the surface and is overgrown with corals and encrusting marine life.

The forward section of the hold is packed with round canisters about the size of 30-gallon drums. These are mines. This hold also contains encrusted carbine rifles, ammunition, stacks of helmets and gas masks, and depth charges. The bridge floorboards have disappeared, but the helm and the brass ring of the wheel (marine worms ate the wood, leaving only the brass) are present and laying on their sides. The galley has pots, pans, bottles, cups, dishes, claret glasses, a coal burning stove, and other utensils. There is also a small radio room with equipment still in place. The engine room has been protected from heavy silting because the skylights are closed. The engine and winch remain in fine shape and the brass gauges below the engine room catwalk in the boiler area are still readable. The ship's stack is missing and sits on the reef along the starboard.

The forward holds contain assorted electrical parts and fixtures. It is possible to swim from the center hold to the forward hold as the partition between decks is gone. The most notable pieces of cargo are three large airplane engines in the forward hold. The boatswain's locker in the bow contains some beautiful storm lanterns and a taff rail log any seasoned navigator would love to have a look at. The lightbulb in the locker is still intact in the overhead light fixture.

Francis Toribiong found a small bugle in the silt on the ocean floor along the starboard. This is an odd and unique piece of memorabilia. It is possible the ship's bell will also be found here and will provide positive identification of the wreck.

4

Safety

Emergency Services for Palau

The only recompression facility in the western Pacific is located on Guam. It is the SRF Guam Recompression Chamber 671-339-7143. It is located near the ship repair facility on the main Naval Station.

Guam Hospitals

Guam Memorial Hospital
Emergency Room
Tamuning
646-8104

Naval Hospital
Agana Heights
344-9232

Diving Physician, Guam

George P. Macris, M.D.
637-4179
Tel/Fax: 637-4385

Palau Hospital

Medical Emergency
Koror: 488-1422

Dangerous Marine Animals

Few places have as much diversity of fish and invertebrates as the Palau Islands. Yet, few marine-related injuries are reported every year. A little common sense and respect for wild animals goes a long way in preventing any sort of mishap on the reef.

Jellyfish. The Palau waters have many jellyfish. Most are the mastgias. They can be directed away from a diver by pushing them away with their bulbous top. Their lower sections and tentacles deliver the sting. Some people have mild reactions to jellyfish stings, others have severe allergic reactions. Normally, meat tenderizer will neutralize the sting of a jellyfish. See a physician for any problems. In the marine lakes, the jellyfish have lost their need to sting, having formed a symbiotic relationship with algae for food. Ask a guide first, but these jellyfish can be handled without harm.

Sea urchins. This critter is the scourge of divers and swimmers worldwide. The victim normally kneels on or puts a hand or finger on an urchin. The animal's brittle spines break off and its puncture can be immediately painful. It usually takes a few weeks for the spines to work their way out.

Antibiotic cream will keep the wound from infecting. For major punctures, see a physician.

Scorpionfish, stonefish. These animals camouflage themselves easily and injuries are also normally the result of an accidental meeting of diver and fish. These stings should not be taken lightly. Severe allergic reactions have occurred in some victims. See a doctor immediately or go to the emergency room at the hospital. Pain can sometimes be eased by submerging the wound in hot water.

Lionfish. The rear spines of the lionfish can also deliver a painful sting. The intensity of pain from these wounds has been likened to that of childbirth. Do not tease or attempt to handle these beautiful fish. They can strike with lightning speed.

Crown-of-thorns starfish. The acanthaster can deliver a painful wound that can fester and become severely infected. Treat this wound at once and see a doctor. An old island cure is to put the mouth of the same animal that punctured you on the wound and it will suck out its poison. You can try this, but see a doctor too. The complications from a crown-of-thorns wound can be extensive if not treated properly.

Eels. Eels are normally shy and reclusive. Do not harass them or put your hand into any holes of the ship or the coral. Their teeth tilt backwards so they can deliver a wound that will shred skin.

Barracuda. These mean-looking fish are normally curious but not a threat. They are sometimes attracted to shiny objects. If visibility is low, stay out of the water when barracuda are present. Do not spearfish when they are around.

Sharks. There are few documented cases of shark attacks on divers. Most attacks in Micronesia result from a diver spearfishing. The sharks smell the blood in the water and pick up the vibes of the wounded fish and become competitive and aggressive. Normally, sharks will come to look at a diver and leave. If one hangs around too long or starts to make quick movements and displays with its fins, leave the area and get out of the water.

Appendix 1

Diver Guidelines for Protecting Reefs*

1. Maintain proper buoyancy control, and avoid over-weighting.
2. Use correct weight belt position to stay horizontal, i.e., raise the belt above your waist to elevate your feet/fins, and move it lower toward your hips to lower them.
3. Use your tank position in the backpack as a balance weight, i.e., raise your backpack on the tank to lower your legs, and lower the backpack on the tank to raise your legs.
4. Watch for buoyancy changes during a dive trip. During the first couple of days, you'll probably breathe a little harder and need a bit more weight than the last few days.
5. Be careful about buoyancy loss at depth; the deeper you go the more your wet suit compresses, and the more buoyancy you lose.
6. Photographers must be extra careful. Cameras and equipment affect buoyancy. Changing f-stops, framing a subject, and maintaining position for a photo often conspire to prohibit the ideal "no-touch" approach on a reef. So, when you must use "holdfasts," choose them intelligently.
7. Avoid full leg kicks when working close to the bottom and when leaving a photo scene. When you inadvertently kick something, stop kicking! Seems obvious, but some divers either semi-panic or are totally oblivious when they bump something.
8. When swimming in strong currents, be extra careful about leg kicks and handholds.
9. Attach dangling gauges, computer consoles, and octopus regulators. They are like miniature wrecking balls to a reef.
10. Never drop boat anchors onto a coral reef.

*Condensed from "Diver Guidelines" by Chris Newbert © Oceanica 1991. Reprinted with permission of Oceanica and Chris Newbert. If you are interested in more information or in helping Oceanica preserve our ocean realm, please write in Oceanica, 342 West Sunset, San Antonio, Texas 78209, USA.

Appendix 2

Dive Operators

The list below is included as a service to the reader. The list is as accurate as possible at the time of printing. This list does not constitute an endorsement of these facilities. If operators/owners wish to be included in future reprints/editions, please contact Pisces Books, P.O. Box 2608, Houston, Texas 77252-2608.

Live-aboards

Micronesian Yachts
Ocean Hunter
Book through See & Sea Travel
　Service Inc.
50 Francisco St., Suite 205
San Francisco, California 94133
Tel: 415-434-3400
FAX: 415-434-3409

Palau Aggressor
Aggressor Fleet
P.O. Drawer K
Morgan City, LA 70381
FAX: 504-384-0817
Live-aboard services with
photo and diving services

The Palau Pacific Resort provides first-class accommodations.

Land Based Dive Operators

There are about 15 dive operators in Palau that cater mainly to Japanese dive groups. There are also a number of locally owned dive operations that primarily serve European and Western visitors. Listed are the operations, most of which are staffed by local guides who speak English. Note that many of the FAX numbers are the same. For many Palau businesses, the faxes go to a central communications station, and businesses are notified when a fax arrives.

Carp Island Corporation
Attn: Johnny Kishigawa
P.O. Box 5
Koror, Palau 96940
FAX: 680-488-1725
Diving tours to the walls and reefs and a cozy, unique Rock Island Resort

Fish N' Fins Limited
Toribiong Company
Attn: Francis Toribiong
P.O. Box 142
Koror, Palau 96940
FAX: 680-488-1725
Local guides with dives to walls, reefs, and World War II shipwrecks. Dive shop adjoins the Palau Marina Hotel. NAUI courses available.

NECO Marine Corp.
Attn: Shallum Etpison
P.O. Box 129
Koror, Palau 96940
FAX: 680-488-2880
Local guides provide trips to Palau's popular sites. PADI courses available.

Sam's Tour Service
Attn: Sam Scott
P.O. Box 428
Koror, Palau 96940
FAX: 680-488-1471
Locally owned business has personalized tours for small groups to dive sites. Hotel packages can be arranged.

Splash Divers
Attn: Palau Pacific Resort
P.O. Box 308
Koror, Palau 96940
FAX: (Guam Office) 671-649-4957
Trips to local dive sites. Introductory courses and open water courses available.

Index

A large cotton candy coral nestles with a broad sea anemone along the wall.

 **Pisces Books™**

Be sure to check out these other great books from Pisces:

Great Reefs of the World
Watching Fishes: Understanding Coral Reef Fish Behavior
Skin Diver Magazine's Book of Fishes, 2nd Edition
Shooting Underwater Video: A Complete Guide to the Equipment and Techniques for
    Shooting, Editing, and Post-Production

Diving and Snorkeling Guides to:

Australia: Coral Sea and Great Barrier Reef
Australia: Southeast Coast and Tasmania
The Bahamas: Family Islands and Grand Bahama
The Bahamas: Nassau and New Providence Island 2nd Edition
Belize
Bonaire
The British Virgin Islands
The Cayman Islands 2nd Edition
The Channel Islands
Cozumel, 2nd Edition
Curaçao
Fiji
Florida's East Coast, 2nd Edition
The Florida Keys, 2nd Edition
The Great Lakes
The Hawaiian Islands, 2nd Edition
Northern California and the Monterey Peninsula, 2nd Edition
The Pacific Northwest
Roatan and Honduras' Bay Islands
Texas
The Turks and Caicos Islands
The U.S. Virgin Islands, 2nd Edition

Available from your favorite dive shop, bookstore, or directly from the publisher: Pisces Books™, a division of Gulf Publishing Company, Book Division, Dept. AD, P.O. Box 2608, Houston, Texas 77252-2608. (713) 520-4444.

Include purchase price plus $4.95 for shipping and handling. IL, NJ, PA, and TX residents add appropriate tax.

The sun sets over a tiny, shrub-covered islet near Peleliu's harbor in southern Palau.